Brown Restless Green

poems by

Jannett Highfill

Finishing Line Press
Georgetown, Kentucky

Brown Restless Green

ACKNOWLEDGMENTS

Bluffs Literary Magazine: "Drinking Morning Coffee On a Day My Calendar
is Covered with Meetings"
Escape Into Life: "The Edge of the Desert"
The Hardy Review: "As Long As the Light Lasts"
Ordinary Time: "By June," "A Fallacy of Composition," "Afternoon Before
New Year's Eve"
A Prairie Journal: "Commute"
The Six-Legged Creature: "Ashtray," "Gyp Flats: 53 Month Drought," "South of
Freedom, Oklahoma," "Thanksgiving," and "Homesick"
Tar River Poetry: "East Dennis"
Thin Air: "Life Work"

Publisher: Leah Huete de Maines
Editor: Christen Kincaid
Cover Art: William Weber and Ty Patterson
Author Photo: Regina Barker, Regina Barker Photography
Cover Design: Elizabeth Maines McCleavy

Order online: www.finishinglinepress.com
also available on amazon.com

Author inquiries and mail orders:
Finishing Line Press
PO Box 1626
Georgetown, Kentucky 40324
USA

Table of Contents

For Virgie, Andy, and Becky

Drinking Morning Coffee on a Day My Calendar is Covered with Meetings

The balcony is carpeted in helicopters, paper-thin tan ones, single winged, as big as your thumb, twice as many smaller double winged green ones, spring green by definition. Standing here, looking up, you wouldn't know

the neighborhood has a single maple, red, silver, black, striped, or any other, you wouldn't imagine we have wind currents strong enough two or three stories up, whipping between and around all these apartment buildings.

My neighbor Patricia says these things sprout in concrete. Guess I'll see since I have neither potted plant nor window box. In the fourteen minutes I have with my coffee this morning there are no seedpod landings, only two

fly-aways, but the whole balcony floor is restless. I know one in a thousand successfully germinates—and that's the point—but today you'd think it was the flittering, dancing, skipping end over end. And thus I flutter off to work.

East Dennis

The summer after Mama died
my Aunt Belle snapping beans
or shaking sand out of towels

meticulously logged my discoveries:
hermit crab and sand dollar, ribbon-
weed kelp, phosphorescent jellyfish,
and, once, a crimson sea-star,

for Dad and Uncle Charlie, arriving
at twilight on Friday. Dark or not
streetlights were for elsewhere—
Boston or China. After supper

the four of us walked to the beach
through the stillness and rising mist
or under the large few stars.

Crow Time

I drove over a crow
just after noon Thanksgiving day.
Nothing for me to do but keep driving—

couldn't just then change lanes, no
time to stop, no shoulder.
Ok, so perhaps a bit of tarpaper,

but in my rearview mirror
I saw it fly up and perch on the sign
for Three Sisters Park.

Crow playing chicken with a car?
I don't believe a deaf-blind
wild creature would survive for long.

At home for the whole summer
and fall a crow surveyed
the block it seemed to own

from the neighbor's scrub mimosa,
hopped in front of anyone on foot
to caw and scold.

Cars, however, it avoided—
exploiting the straight-forward
advantages of flight.

Now driving on between
river and park I wonder what bird
lives on the highway by choice.

On the highway.
Nothing I did—
but this time it survived my journey.

Carved in Stone

The tourist bus pulls up to Grasmere Church.
They're selling paving stones and we buy one,

meaning 375 pounds for a square of cement
we'll never see on a path down the green hill
between church and garden, today daffodils.

You suggest "engraved"
while I favor "Mount Abora."

Simple line art is available, 35 pounds,
although not the watering can

Dorothy christened "Kubla"
the afternoon Wordsworth told Coleridge
to waft his dream into the kitchen stove.

We choose initials, as a compromise.

Ashtray

Its bowl is two thumb-
  prints
 wide and etched
with a circle of
  six doves.

Smoke rises heaven-
  ward
 with the birds.
I write "me" in the
  ashes.

Abide

He'd say his idea of a garden
is a cricket for luck and a killing frost
after mowing the grass and hoeing
the beds along the sidewalk and
around the patio so I wouldn't have to.

Now I've let the weeds get head-
high and as fat as me. I could let
contingency take all of them.
A hard freeze kills with an even hand.

In this neighborhood not a soul
would notice. And the one who'd care
won't be off rehab before winter.

Gyp Flats: 53 Month Drought

Sandburs and stickers choose small children,
the unwary, and the hard-pressed
indiscriminately. Locals keep
to the road from the time they can walk
or if that is not possible
find another way to pay their respects.

Sandburs are ankle-
biters. Stickers grow
higher than work boots
on a grown man;
they're harder on hands,
a thousand barbs per
pull off a shoelace.

This county was homesteaded a hundred
and twenty years ago. Roads run parallel
ruts in grassland and gypsum. Even if they
were the least troublesome of heat rash, poison
sumac, and red ants, sandburs didn't hurt less then
than now. Summers children were barefoot,
except Sunday.
Only the men might have leather work gloves.

Rain now. Day after day,
pop-up storms, steamy
rainbows, scorching sun
gaps in the downpour.
What is overflowering
to abandoned ungrazeable prairie?

The Last Thing I Say

to "goodnight" and sagging bones
dragging themselves away from ten minutes hanging
on the edge of the bed I say after
the room's two naked bulbs are shut down
to street light framing the window,
a knife edge under the door,
when the long cough has taken up residence
in the chair next door so I can sleep
and the words
I should have choked on morning and evening
have settled like dust—
the hard cheap quarrelsome words with legs
and orange makeup said and said and said
as if to control by incantation
my lips bruising—
and the old man wanting nothing of me except health,
my resilient health that I cannot give
or share or trade for amiable companionship
whether I would or not who sat silently
on my bed and waited for a silence I did not offer
and do not offer even as he goes out
and I am talking to the dust
and the frame and the knife edge, and maybe
a small part of himself and no dreams.

A Fallacy of Composition

I get confused.

I think the five-point brown leaves
on the creek bank in Lower Bradley Park
were arranged by texture and value

on a muralist's scale.
I've seen the bas-relief,
miniaturized, sterling or 14 karat,

available on Michigan Avenue.
The logo of my grocery-store bank
features a maple leaf, perfectly symmetrical.

But it's an ordinary random oak leaf
I pick up now,
to hold onto something,

carry it home
to let it dry on a shelf in the kitchen.

Carry this increasingly frail fractal
conflation of process and design
with me through winter.

As Long as the Light Lasts

Howard carries breakfast's leftover coffee in a glass jar to the work site,
drinks it with his lunch lukewarm. Erma drinks water, by season

frozen overnight or boiled for a thermos. They take apart buildings
for scrap, board by board, nail by nail—outbuildings on farms or small

houses in tiny towns, no place to pick up a Coke or sandwich if they
wanted to, which they don't. Did I say they've been on Social Security

for seventeen years? They sell the windows or copper pipe, use
the rest to build storage sheds, miniature red barns. They knock off

work about four to sit out the heat of the day, or get home before dark
at the other end of the year. They are devotees of the public library.

Between extremes they garden after supper, as long as the light lasts.

Paid Announcement

From the reaches of space:
Unretouched
time exposure shows
Echo I
communications satellite
(long line)
crossing the heavens right
to left.
Shorter lines are stars
"in motion."

Bell Telephone System
Journal of Political Economy

Patience

He sits in the blue chair until the upholstered buttons
pop off and stainless steel wing nuts drop from its innards
littering the floor and still he sits in the chair.

Pneumonia is a patient thing, the old man's friend
in the old country proverb. He wears a pleasant green robe
each day he's sick, a field green that never burns,

a green man in a blue chair for a season, spring,
and another, summer. He sits his back to the window,
establishing his own background and foreground.

For a city man he's watched the seasons, gathered
their pace and rhythms into himself, gathered the light
in his eyes. He sleeps easily through short nights.

Thanksgiving

The horizon is sunset-gray below
receding snow skiffs;

one furrow in the water flickers;
a north wind stirs up and out of the duck

blind poised where the river
spreads lake-size,

a plywood box nailed to a platform on stilts,
water lapping in.

I want to put duck-blind photos in galleries
with a hearty artist statement

playing for mortal stakes
and a modest stash of green.

Only three days of duck season left
but no one goes hungry if a hunt fails.

I should be ungrateful
my daily bread comes otherwise?

Layover

A small shop in the airport
sells cloisonné wise men:
four and a half inches tall,
bright colored enamel in brass outlines
almost stained glass in three dimensions.
Dozens of them.
I'm buying soda and almonds.
The customer in front of me has
carefully chosen one of each color
combination, set them out on the counter
like chessmen on a game board.
The customer and the clerk
say a few words over the chosen ones
scanned and then crinkled into tissue paper.
Wish I'd checked restless
with the family gifts an airport back.

Eagle the Color of Grass

Eagle carrying a fish along the tree line,
the river is almost clear of ice. The old
season's browns, golds, greenish-tans cut

through the snow where someone has walked
ahead, someone and a dog. I wonder if
Warren would have walked with me today,

cold but sunny. But I don't even know
how to ask the question. Which Warren?
Not the last few years when he wasn't himself.

Before.

I could never guess whether he'd leave
his Sunday afternoon of writing and reading for
the river, gulls, and barges—he appreciated

both nuisance bird and forthright commerce
but this river is not his ocean. On his best
day here he might have said the grass

deconstructs the palette of F.W. Benson's
Osprey and Fish—completely ignoring
floating ice or pelican flock. Overlooking

too the omnipresent haze where the river
bends towards the east.

Today I don't know whether to miss him,
the unsettled not knowing,
whether he would look up for anything

or let me tell him about it. Today an eagle
flew over my head, down the tree line,
into the haze and sun.

Homesick

How long does she hold her body tight as a vise around
her desire to be where she will be in twenty-six hours?
By what other means can she know the value of home?

How can she remove herself from Corfu so not even
the dust of her breath remains? How can she be home
if even that much of herself remains behind, if she so much

as remembers this place where for half an hour—
translucent sea, glass of water and lemon slice, poppy
floating in an ashtray—she was happy?

Art is Death:

A stay against

Green scarecrow
Red nose   Red mouth

Black top hat and frock coat
so frayed black is blue
in the creases

Joyce, the downstairs neighbor,
saying the green man is Warren's shadow

Fall Art Fair poster—
six weeks inescapable
yard sign, billboard, broadside

Each time Warren
staring at the scarecrow-ghost
quizzical look in his eyes

puzzled by neighborly
meaning and meanness

Both neighbors dead now

All Hallows Eve.

Commute

I don't do boredom
and there is an abundance
of routes between work
and home. Perhaps
I should pick a new one
every evening,
the last of my daily
executive decisions—
when to go for coffee
(twice)
whether to delete
or archive my email,
how to laugh off
my boss's drollery
of the day. But
I'm tired after work,
just want to forget,
until waiting at the light,
Northmoor at Knoxville,
an oak tree twice
as tall as the light standard
fronting it transfixes me,
this tree,
this silhouette listing
south against blue
in summer
and black in winter
and once a year a harvest moon.
The tree gives nothing,
leaving me nothing to decide.

Resources

My father would have said it is a question of resources.

I have a chair, faded cabbage rose upholstery. Today
except for eating and dressing I'm here, at a north window,

looking at the whole world. Single trees here and there
grace the buildings next door and across the street,
some taller than two or three stories, some just above

human height. The invisible changeable sun favors

moment to moment particular branches and leaves;
a gust of wind disrupts the pattern and variation.

Today I sit and watch what is enacted as if
it were a ceremony. I know there must be sparrows
and squirrels, but there is nothing to bring them

here to my window. Of course, I remember when I
could have gone to them, or to the grocery store,

or the opera, Mozart or Puccini, when I gave most
days, eight or sixteen hours, to a job I loved. Now
the circumference of my life is this room, the extent

of my venturing is this chair. The last question is whether
I can sit here without indulging myself, restless or bored.

Today the air is white, then the grass, then the street.
Today the sun sets behind the northernmost chimney
of the red brick apartments by the railroad track.

Today the invisible sun reflects on an expanse
of clouds, brushing a swath of green on the heavens.

South of Freedom, Oklahoma

Bad enough my brother takes off from the plant
the Sunday before Christmas,
picks me up at the Wichita airport, and we drive
three and a half hours southwest
to walk the fences
of a field growing nothing but taxes
that's been in the family
since 1903 and going nowhere—
bad enough to come just because it's been a while,

but even worse in freezing rain.
Every step shatters ice; with every gust of wind
a top-heavy weed snaps.
Ice wouldn't hurt winter wheat if there were any
and if it knocks down the Johnson grass that's
all to the good. The danger's to us.
On the long companionable drive back
we talk about everything but selling out.

Tenaya Lake, Mount Conness, California

Ansel Adams
in 500 diabolical pieces.

Too hard is strict
unreconstructed frustration.

Why did Michael Adams,
executor, trustee,
let Mattel do it?

25 or 50 pieces would
finesse kids into appreciation.

Legacy grandeur is worse
than cardboard advertisement.

Almost Free

A thousand nights too hot to rest but not
to dream and one when a cold front and mourning
doves tell a story, or just the beginning, "Once
upon this time," and my cramped crabbed
dream *lost hostage in a maze of heat lightning*
dissipates like a cloud. Maybe the heat
will break with the dawn and I'll have something to do,
meaning something I want to do.
Thunder and dove song before the alarm.
Furious rain scrubs the window.

Next Door to the Mt. Pisgah Baptist Church

A crow, the master of the parking lot,
raises Cain with those of the saints eager
for a good seat in the sanctuary or late
for rehearsal with the golden age choir.
Hailing raccoons, squirrels, conies,
sparrows, a dove, he regally holds court

owns everything in sight; he knows I'm here
by myself behind safety glass, sees nothing
surprising in that. He's sure the bells ring
at his command, that he could call me out.
In the sunlight his throat is purple and blue.

The Edge of the Desert

1. International Conference, Casablanca

Soldiers stand at street corners, rifles like sashes across their chests,
while foreign scholars declaim *decentralized democracy*
versus non-inflationary monetary policy.
The merchants of the *souq* talk fast, but do not smile at tourists.
The streets are Mercedes or mule-cart wide, the air
manure and diesel. The dolls are handmade for westerners so
much *maroquinerie*. Leather. (About thirty-five euros.)
Jellaba—the full-length cotton garment worn by the Berber.
The doll the economist chooses is an empty
jellaba: hood but no head, sleeves but no hands, robe but no feet.
The emperor has no clothes, the *jellaba* no Berber. See,
molded leather over an invisibility.
Call an International Conference: *Marketing the Doll*
to the Wickedly Lost. Could someone sell us a soul?

2. Outside Marrakech

A man gets out of a minivan,
sits on a stone curb at the edge
of the desert, doesn't see the huge
red sun on the sand behind him.
He's reading *The Lonely Planet* but on that
page it doesn't say "look up,"
"look around you."

Afternoon Before New Year's Eve

Snow.
Settling calm and content
to work from home tomorrow
having gathered in
apples, spinach, yellow peppers, cherry tomatoes, bananas,
every fruit and vegetable out of season
within two thousand miles.
Working the year-end
computations,
preliminary reckoning against
pausing before
the artificial day of hope:
parades, football games, and fresh baked bread
from Grandmother's recipe.
Every grain of wheat has a heart
in our health-nut flour.
An avocado sliced open,
the halves side by side
for another heart.
Snow and the accidents of the Gregorian calendar
for a family half-day, day, and another
immeasurable year.

Homing

Imagine I'm a pigeon at work.
Imagine that.

For three semesters
the provost's pre-strategic planning process memo
muddied the break room bulletin board.

One of us confirms pigeons find their way home
by following rivers and landmarks.
By sight that is.
But if released with hoods
they still find their way.

To their home cage.
Pigeons, my colleague says,
have senses we don't know of.
One of us ran those experiments.
Our shop.

Life Work

It's my life's work: a transparent sea capsule,
a circular platform, eight-foot diameter
encased in a Lucite globe, eight feet above
the water line eight feet below. The thing is
no matter how heavy the sea is the globe
shifts with the waves, the platform staying
perfectly still. Gyroscopes. I won't tell
you how. Won't tell how many companies
are after me for it, oil companies, drillers,
salvage operations, a few pirates. But I've
built only seven of them, offer an excursion

for one of the better cruise lines. For 500
dollars I'll tender you out to a platform and
leave you there, alone. Take myself over
the horizon so all you see is water on all sides.
I give you a radio of course; you can talk
to me driving the boat anytime. Most people
stay about 15 minutes although you can stay
as long as your ship is in port. I get all ages;
the younger ones have slept in the pyramids
at Giza, the cave at Lascaux, the Creswell Crags
and talk about brain training and power.

Yes, the platform is steady enough for wheel
chairs, get a fair number of them. I always
sell out even though the cruise ship line
never advertises my excursion and I have
the same contract all its concessionaires do.
My bones are getting too creaky to run
the business much longer; can hardly bear
to think who my son will sell out to when he
gets the chance. But I can't leave it to anyone
else, or smash the mechanism, or burn the
plans. The young are hard to talk to

customers or not. The old ones visit with me like nothing but horizon is an everyday occurrence for them, or soon will be.

Jannett Highfill is a poet and economist living in Wichita Kansas. She has two poetry chapbooks, *A Constitution of Silence* and *Light Blessings Drifting Together*, as well as poems in such journals as *Escape Into Life*, *The Hardy Review*, and *Tar River Poetry*. Her poetry is especially indebted to the Grandview Hotel Poets of Peoria Illinois as well as her many colleagues and friends at Bradley University. Her economic research interests are in applied microeconomics, the fields ranging from municipal recycling to student effort models and instructional design. She is coauthor of *A Tempered and Humane Economy: Markets, Families, and Behavioral Economics* which uses the latter concepts to understand certain micro questions of interpersonal relationships and macro questions such as those related to poverty and wealth.

www.ingramcontent.com/pod-product-compliance
Lightning Source LLC
LaVergne TN
LVHW041328080426
835513LV00008B/641